CACTUSES
of Big Bend National Park

S0-AIR-443

NUMBER THIRTY-EIGHT

Corrie Herring Hooks Series

Douglas B. Evans

CACTUSES
of Big Bend National Park

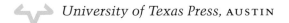 University of Texas Press, AUSTIN

All photographs by Doris and Doug Evans unless otherwise noted.

Requests for permission to reproduce material from this work should be sent to Permissions, University of Texas Press, Box 7819, Austin, TX 78713-7819.

◉ The paper used in this publication meets the minimum requirements of American National Standard for Information Sciences—Permanence of Paper for Printed Library Materials, ANSI Z39.48-1984.

Designed by Ellen McKie

LIBRARY OF CONGRESS CATALOGING-IN-PUBLICATION DATA

Evans, Douglas B.
    Cactuses of Big Bend National Park / Douglas B. Evans. — 1st University of Texas Press ed.
        p.   cm. — (Corrie Herring Hooks series ; no. 38)
    Includes index.
    ISBN 0-292-72098-x (cloth). — ISBN 0-292-72099-8 (pbk.)
    1. Cactus—Texas—Big Bend National Park—Identification.
2. Cactus—Texas—Big Bend National Park—Pictorial works.
3. Big Bend National Park (Tex.) I. Title. II. Series.
QK495.C11E95 1998
583'.56'09764932—dc21   98-10157

Contents

LIVING ROCK CACTUSES

Thick fleshy stems underground, flattened top
even with ground surface; up to about 5 inches
in diameter. Triangular tubercles are warty and
fissured. No areoles; no spines. Flowers and
fruits on new growth near tip of stem.

TOPFLOWER CACTUSES

Stems solitary or branched, sometimes forming clumps, up to about 8 inches long. Spines
usually straight, up to about 2 inches long.
Flowers and fruits on new growth at tips of
stems. Fruits fleshy at maturity.

STOUT-SPINED CACTUSES

The Big Bend species have solitary globose to
hemispherical stems with prominent ribs and
stout, curved spines. Flowers are large and
showy and occur near the growing tips of stems.

The Genus *Echinocereus*   24
HEDGEHOG CACTUSES

Cylindrical stems may be solitary or profusely branched, forming dense clusters or mounds. The tubercles are on the 5 to 12 ribs. The stem surface is obscured by the dense covering of spines. Flowers are usually large and showy. Flowers and fruits occur well below tips of stems.

The Genus *Echinomastus*   33
PINEAPPLE CACTUSES

Egg-shaped stems to about 6 inches long. Dense spines obscure stem surfaces. Flowers usually white to light pink with traces of tan or green.

The Genus *Epithelantha*   37
BUTTON CACTUSES

Tiny globular to cylindroid stems up to about 1 inch in diameter, rarely to 2 inches long. Minute whitish spines completely obscure stem surface. Tiny flowers occur on tip of stems. Mature fruits are bright red.

The Genus *Ferocactus*   41
BARREL CACTUSES

The usually solitary columnar stems have several prominent ribs. Flowers and fruits occur near tips of stems. The lone Big Bend species grows to about a foot tall and has prominent tubercles and very long, flexible hooked spines.

Acknowledgments

Cactuses of Big Bend National Park is based   « **ix** »
on numerous scientific books and journals, too many to cite
individually. I owe much credit and gratitude to these many
plant taxonomists who work to create order out of the chaos
known as Cactaceae. Thanks to Dr. Barton Warnock for his
wise counsel, encouragement, and review of the earliest drafts.
Thanks to Dr. Mike Powell of Sul Ross State University and to
Kenneth Heil of San Juan College for guiding my research in the
right directions. Thanks to Carl Robinson of the Big Bend
Natural History Association and to the staff of the University of
Texas Press for their steadfast support and professional manage-
ment of the project. Thanks to Linda Gregonis for her much
appreciated editorial expertise. Thanks to many dear friends,
especially Anne Bellamy, for their encouragement and for
sharing many cherished Big Bend experiences and memories.
And the most special thanks to Doris, my partner in life who
shares my love for the Big Bend country, for her loving reassur-
ance, her companionship on the trail, her talent for spotting the
smallest obscure cactuses, and her photography skills. Thanks
to you all. But I bear the ultimate responsibility for the end
result; any and all deficiencies are mine.

CACTUSES
of Big Bend National Park

Introduction

Many of us who visit and explore Big Bend
National Park are fascinated by those strange and interesting
plants of the cactus family We enjoy searching for them,
photographing them, and trying to identify them. But this can
be difficult and frustrating for a variety of reasons: some cactus
species are uncommon, some are very obscure, and many occur
only in remote sections of the park. To add further to our
confusion, there is much disagreement among cactus specialists, "cactologists," regarding the classification and naming of
many cactuses. Many species are very similar with subtle
distinctions apparent only to the practiced eye of an expert.
And some cactus species hybridize, so there may be gradations
between one species and another. The purpose of this book is
to help you, the park visitor who may not be a trained botanist,
identify and enjoy the cactuses you might encounter while
driving and hiking in Big Bend National Park.

My own fascination with plants began at a very young age.
As an "NPS Brat" (both of my parents retired from National
Park Service), I grew and matured in an environment where
love and appreciation of the natural world didn't have to be
learned; it was, simply, *natural.* My particular interest in the
plants of Big Bend National Park flourished during my years as
this park's second chief park naturalist. Years later, following
my retirement from the NPS Southwest Regional Office in
Santa Fe, my wife Doris accepted a position teaching children of
park employees at San Vicente School, which is located at the
park's headquarters at Panther Junction. For the next eight years
we explored, studied, photographed, and interpreted the Big
Bend country. These experiences reflect our passion for sharing
our love of the natural and cultural values of this great outdoor
classroom with others, particularly children. These thoughts
and feelings inspired us to pursue the publication of this book.

We usually use the common names of plants, but it is

important when discussing cactuses to be aware of their scientific names, too. Since scientific nomenclature is more systematic and consistent, it allows us to be more precise and to understand the relationships of the various species of cactus.

Scientific names are universal throughout the world. Botanists in Asia or Europe, for example, use the same scientific names as we do in the Americas. In the scientific system, members of a plant family are grouped according to similarity of characters, particularly of the flowers, into a number of genera (singular: genus). Each genus is divided into species. So the scientific name is a *binomial*, or two-word name, consisting of the name of the genus and the name of the species. Some species are further divided into varieties. Occasionally it will be to our benefit to refer to varieties, but to the greatest extent possible we will try to avoid them.

While discussing nomenclature, let's consider the old question: which is correct, *cacti* or *cactuses?* My answer is: it depends on which language you are communicating in. If in Latin, then *cacti* is definitely correct. However, if you're conversing or writing in American English, as I am doing in this book, then *cactuses* is perfectly acceptable, and I personally prefer it.

Finally, a word about the preservation of cactuses and other natural resources in Big Bend and other national parks. There are two fundamental reasons why every visitor should not remove or damage plants in the national parks: to do so is both immoral and illegal. National parks are established as preserves where native plants and animals can survive and thrive in their natural habitats. We have no right to deprive them of that opportunity. Also, the resources of national parks belong to all of us—equally! The removal of plants, or any other natural or historical resources, is simply theft: stealing from us and our fellow citizens. Unfortunately, laws are necessary to dissuade some people from committing this sort of theft. Federal regulations prohibiting the theft of these resources from your national parks are strictly enforced. If you should witness other visitors stealing your cactuses from your national park, please report such crime to the nearest ranger station immediately.

Cactuses of Big Bend National Park

Big Bend and the Chihuahuan Desert

A nearly continuous arid region extends through western North America from eastern Washington State southward to the Mexican state of Puebla. This irregular area of some 500,000 square miles is generally known as the Great North American Desert. Four distinct deserts have been described within this vast region, based on geographical and biological factors. These are the Great Basin Desert, the Mohave Desert, the Sonoran Desert, and the Chihuahuan Desert. Some plants and animals are endemic to their particular desert; that is, they don't occur in any of the other deserts. Many organisms, however, are found in two or more desert regions. Big Bend National Park was established to preserve the outstanding example of the Chihuahuan Desert in the United States.

About 90 percent of the Chihuahuan Desert is in Mexico with the remaining 10 percent in West Texas, southern New Mexico, and a bit in extreme southeastern Arizona. The Chihuahuan Desert is a high desert, the average elevation being above 3,500 feet. The lowest elevation, less than 1,500 feet, is along the Rio Grande in South Texas. Hot in summer, the Chihuahuan Desert can be cold in winter. Summer temperatures over 100°F are common. Freezing temperatures can be expected during many nights each winter, and some days do not get above freezing. The Chihuahuan Desert is primarily a shrub desert characterized by a variety of yuccas (*Yucca* sp.), agaves (*Agave* sp.), cenizas (*Leucophyllum* sp.), ocotillo (*Fouquieria splendens*), candelilla (*Euphorbia antisyphlitica*), and many others. Nonetheless, the cactus family (Cactaceae) is well represented in the Chihuahuan Desert. This book describes most of those that are known to occur in Big Bend National Park.

Meet the Cactus Family

The first step in getting to know the cactuses is to answer that most basic question: what is a cactus? And, at the same time, we can consider a number of other plants that are commonly referred to as cactuses but are not.

The cactuses belong to their very own family: Cactaceae. They are of relatively recent origin, having evolved in the tropical and arid environments of western America during the past 20,000 years. This is truly an American family of plants; cactuses found in other parts of the world have been transported there from the Americas. Many botanists believe this family's ancestors were closely related to those of the roses. As the desert regions became increasingly arid, those individuals most suited to the heat and drought survived to reproduce and pass those traits on to their offspring. These adaptations distinguish this unique plant family: thick fleshy stems store moisture, a waxy epidermis and the absence of leaves reduce evaporation from the plants, and broad shallow root systems quickly absorb the limited rainfall.

A few cactus species in other regions have leaves. And a few Big Bend species grow tiny vestigial leaves on very young growing stems, but these soon drop off. So it can be said that mature cactuses of the Big Bend country have no leaves. Most have spines, which are borne in a unique structure called an areole. Cactus flowers have many petals and an especially large number of stamens.

Yuccas, agaves, and ocotillos are sometimes mistakenly called cactuses by novices to the desert. Note, however, that these species all have leaves. The yuccas and agaves have large sharply pointed leaves, and their three-part flowers reveal them to be in the agave family, Agavaceae; plants in this family are closely related to lilies and amaryllis. The long, slender, spiny stems of the ocotillo are frequently bare, but they become lush green with leaves following rains. The ocotillo belongs to its own family: Fouquieriaceae.

YUCCA

OCOTILLO

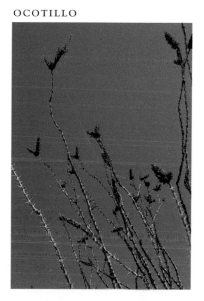

AGAVE

Cactuses of Big Bend National Park

Glossary

Your studies of the cactus family will be easier if you understand the meanings of the following few terms:

Areole
: a specialized spot on the epidermis from which spines and some other structures grow. Areoles are unique to the cactus family.

Central spine
: those spines that grow from the middle of the areoles; sometimes straight, sometimes curved or hooked. They are usually larger and more colorful than the radial spines that grow around the edges of the areoles.

Epidermis
: the protective outer layers of cells of a plant; the "skin."

Genus
: the next level of classification below family; a group of closely related species.

Glochids
: minute hairlike barbed bristles that grow in the areoles of pricklypears and chollas. Glochids (GLAW-kids) usually dislodge easily from the plants, but not from your skin.

Pistil
: the female part of a flower, comprised of the stigma, style, and ovary.

Radial spine
: those spines that grow around the edges of the areoles, surrounding the central spines; they are usually smaller than the centrals.

Rib
: a raised ridge running vertically or spirally along the length of a stem.

Species
: the fundamental level of scientific classification; a homogeneous population of organisms capable of breeding and reproducing fertile offspring.

Spines
: the sharp needlelike structures that grow from areoles.

Stamen	the male part of a flower, comprised of filament and anther; produces pollen.
Stigma	the top of the pistil; the female organ that receives the pollen.
Tubercle	a knob rising from the stem surface, usually bearing an areole.
Variety	a subdivision of a species, varying but slightly from the species. Not all species are divided into varieties.

PARTS OF A CACTUS

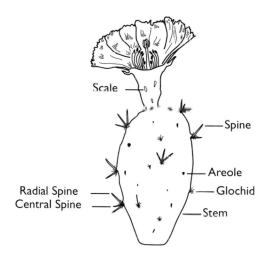

Scale
Spine
Areole
Radial Spine
Central Spine
Glochid
Stem

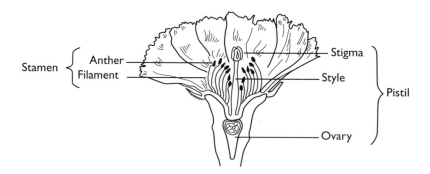

Stamen { Anther / Filament
Stigma
Style
Ovary
Pistil

Cactuses of Big Bend National Park

The Genus *Ariocarpus*
LIVING ROCK CACTUSES

The small genus *Ariocarpus* contains six species, only one of which occurs north of the Rio Grande and in Big Bend National Park.

Living rock cactus
(Ariocarpus fissuratus)

The exposed portion of the living rock stem is flattened even
with the ground surface and is usually about 3 to 5 inches in
diameter. During periods of drought the stems may shrink
below ground level and become covered over with sand and
gravel. The tubercles are deeply fissured and warty, tightly
overlapping each other. The stem is grayish green in color.
Very young plants may have a few spines, but mature plants
have no spines.

The flowers vary from light pink to purple and are $1^{1}/_{2}$ to
2 inches in diameter. They bloom in October and November.
The fruits are green and ripen to brown; at maturity, they are
dry and are embedded in grayish wool.

Living rocks occur below 4,000 feet elevation and are more
commonly found on limestone ridges.

LIVING ROCK CACTUS

The Genus *Ariocarpus*

The Genus *Coryphantha*
TOPFLOWER CACTUSES

The generic name *Coryphantha* means "crest flower" and refers to the position of the flowers on the new growth at the very tips of the stems. It should be noted, however, that this characteristic is not unique to *Coryphantha*; it occurs in other genera as well. The stems may be solitary or branched many times. They do not have ribs, and the tubercles are distinct from each other. The fruits are fleshy at maturity and may be green or red.

Some cactologists do not recognize the genus *Coryphantha* and place these species in the genus *Mammillaria* instead.

The following seven species of topflower cactuses are listed as occurring in Big Bend National Park.

Silverlace cob cactus
(Coryphantha albicolumnaria)

The cylindrical stems of the silverlace cob cactus are commonly solitary, but are occasionally branched into clumps with
up to a dozen stems. The spines are dense, obscuring the stems,
and are white to gray with bluish to reddish tips.

The flowers are pink and up to about 1 1/2 inches across.
They bloom in April and May and following summer showers.
The mature fruits are red and nearly 1 inch long.

SILVERLACE COB CACTUS

The Genus *Coryphantha*

Mountain cob cactus
(Coryphantha dasyacantha)

The solitary stems of the mountain cob cactus reach about 6 inches in height. They are globose when young, but they mature to elongate cylinders. The spines are from about $1/4$ to $1/2$ inch long. The lower spines fall off, revealing the older, dry, hard tubercles and giving the stem its corncob appearance.

The flowers are white to pale pink and about an inch in diameter. They bloom from May through July. The fruits are about $1/2$ inch long, red and fleshy when mature.

Two varieties of mountain cob cactus occur in Big Bend National Park: *C. d.* var. *dasyacantha* has very dense white spines that obscure the surface of the stems. *C. d.* var. *varicolor* has straw-colored spines that are less dense and do not obscure the green stems. These two varieties are very difficult to distinguish in the field.

The mountain cob cactus is uncommon in the foothills surrounding the Chisos Mountains.

MOUNTAIN COB CACTUS. *Photo by Ro Wauer.*

The Genus *Coryphantha*

Duncan cory cactus
(Coryphantha duncanii)

The stems of the Duncan cory cactus are almost always solitary, nearly spherical, and 1 to $2^{1}/_{2}$ inches in diameter. The
white spines are exceedingly dense, completely obscuring the
surfaces of the stems.

The flowers are white to pale pink. They are almost an inch
long, but open to only about $^{1}/_{2}$ inch across. The outer edges of
the petals are slightly fringed. They usually bloom in February
and March. The fruits are bright red when ripe and about
$^{1}/_{2}$ inch long.

The Duncan cory cactus is rare in Big Bend National Park.
It occurs only in crevices in low limestone hills near the
Rio Grande.

DUNCAN CORY CACTUS

The Genus *Coryphantha*

Sea urchin cactus
(Coryphantha echinus)

The stems of the sea urchin cactus are commonly solitary but may occur in clumps. Individual stems are about 4 inches long. The grayish-white spines are very dense, obscuring the surface of the stem. Long, stout, central spines stand straight out from the stem, giving the plant its sea urchin appearance. These central spines are nearly an inch long and are gray, often with black tips.

The spectacular flowers, up to about 3 inches across, have yellow petals and red stamens. The flowers last briefly, only a couple of hours in the afternoon. They bloom from April through August. The green fleshy fruits are about an inch long.

The sea urchin cactus is fairly common at lower elevations in limestone soils.

The Genus *Coryphantha*

SEA URCHIN CACTUS

The Genus *Coryphantha*

Long mamma
(Coryphantha macromeris)

The young stems of long mamma are solitary, but they usually branch many times into large clusters as they mature. Individual stems may reach 6 inches in length. The most conspicuous feature of the stems is the very long, mammarylike tubercles for which the plant is named. The spines are fairly dense, but do not obscure the surface of the stem. They are gray to brown or, occasionally, black.

The pink to purple flowers are about 2 inches across. They bloom from August through September. The egg-shaped fruits are about an inch long and are green at maturity.

Long mamma is fairly common in clay and gravel soils below 4,000 feet in elevation.

LONG MAMMA

Big Bend cory cactus
(Coryphantha ramillosa)

The dark green, solitary, egg-shaped stems grow to about 3 inches in height. They are very similar to the single stems of long mamma. The spines are gray, often with dark tips, and are about 1 inch long.

The flowers are pink to deep rose-purple and are about 2 inches across. They bloom from April through June and after summer showers. The ripe fruits are green but covered with whitish hairlike scales. They are up to an inch in length.

The Big Bend cory cactus is quite rare in Big Bend National Park. It occurs in limestone hills near the Rio Grande.

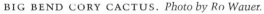

BIG BEND CORY CACTUS. *Photo by Ro Wauer.*

The Genus *Coryphantha*

Spiny star
(Coryphantha vivipara)

The stems of the spiny star may be solitary, but they are commonly branched, sometimes forming mounds. The individual stems are egg-shaped to cylindrical and up to about 5 to 6 inches long. The spines are very dense, obscuring the stems, and are whitish tipped with brown.

The flowers may be pinkish to purple and up to about $1^{1}/_{2}$ inches across. They bloom from June through August. The green fruits are about 1 inch long.

The spiny star cactus occurs in grasslands and juniper woodlands to about 6,000 feet elevation.

SPINY STAR. *Photo by Ro Wauer.*

The Genus *Coryphantha*

The Genus *Echinocactus*
STOUT-SPINED CACTUSES

The stout-spined cactuses of Big Bend
National Park are low, solitary, heavy-bodied
plants. The surface of the stems is hard and
firm. The spines are especially sturdy and
rigid, with prominent heavy central spines
that curve downward.

Turk's head cactus
(Echinocactus horizonthalonius)

The blue-green stem of the Turk's head cactus is usually low and globe-shaped, up to about 6 inches in height. Occasionally it will be cylindrical in form and up to about 12 inches high. The heavy spines are gray; the centrals may be darker and with a reddish tinge.

The flowers, to nearly 3 inches in diameter, are pink to rose red, the tip of each petal irregularly toothed. The flowers sprout from the very tip of the stem. They usually bloom in April and May, but occasional flowers may be found on plants through summer and into fall. The 1-inch fruits dry at maturity and are covered with dense, white, woolly hairs.

Turk's heads are common throughout Big Bend National Park from the Rio Grande up into the Chisos woodlands at 5,500 feet elevation.

The Genus *Echinocactus*

TURK'S HEAD CACTUS

The Genus *Echinocactus*

Horse crippler
(Echinocactus texensis)

Horse crippler stems are commonly low flattened hemispheres, often nearly even with the ground surface. Some may reach a height of about 6 inches and up to 12 inches in diameter. The prominent ribs bear a loose array of extremely heavy and threatening spines for which this cactus was named. The spines are reddish and conspicuously cross-ridged, especially the large, down-curved central spines.

Flower color may vary, but most of the Big Bend flowers are pink with deep red centers. They are about 2 to 2 1/2 inches in diameter. The petals are fringed and feathery at the tips. Horse cripplers may be found in bloom from late March through May. The fruits, about 2 inches long, are bright red and fleshy but become dry and split at maturity.

In Big Bend National Park horse cripplers are uncommon on sandy flats below 3,300 feet elevation. They are usually hidden among grasses. Stories abound in West Texas of livestock and people being injured by stumbling into the menacing spines of this aptly named cactus.

The Genus *Echinocactus*

HORSE CRIPPLER

The Genus *Echinocactus*

The Genus *Echinocereus*
HEDGEHOG CACTUSES

The genus name *Echinocereus* (ee-kine-o-SERious) is derived from the Greek word *echinos*, which means "prickly" or "hedgehog-like," and the Latin *cereus*, meaning "wax candle." The name describes very spiny plants shaped like candles, neatly characterizing this group of cactuses. The stems are conical or cylindrical, either solitary or branched, sometimes forming dense clumps. The stems are ribbed vertically, the ribs supporting rows of tubercles. The spine-bearing areoles occur on the ends of the tubercles. The spines are straight or slightly curved but never hooked.

Hedgehog flowers always occur on old growth of preceding years below the tip of the stem and never on the new growth. They are often large and showy. The fruits are fleshy at maturity, many are edible, and some are delicious. Even the fruits of the hedgehogs are spiny.

Chisos Mountain hedgehog
(Echinocereus chisoensis)

This hedgehog, also known as the Chisos pitaya, was once classified as *E. reichenbachii* var. *chisosensis*. Taxonomists now consider it sufficiently distinct to be classified as a species.

The stems of the Chisos pitaya are either solitary or branched. They average about 5 to 6 inches in height, but may reach as tall as 12 inches. The stems are reddish maroon through much of the year but become green in spring. The spines are dense but do not obscure the surface of the stems. Many areoles bear a conspicuous clump of white cottony material.

The flowers, to 3 inches across, are tricolored: the tips of the petals are pink, the mid-sections white, and the lower portions, forming the centers of the flowers, red. They bloom in March and April. The fruits are greenish red, fleshy, and about 1 to 1 1/2 inches long, also with the white cottony material in the areoles.

The Chisos pitaya is very uncommon in Big Bend National Park and grows in gravelly soils below 2,400 feet elevation.

CHISOS MOUNTAIN HEDGEHOG

Brown-flowered cactus
(Echinocereus chloranthus)

The stems of the brown-flowered cactus are usually single, but they may branch once or twice. They may reach 10 inches in length and 3 inches in diameter. The reddish to brown spines are very dense, obscuring the stems.

The reddish brown funnel-shaped flowers are about an inch long. They bloom from February through May, making this one of the earliest cactuses to bloom in Big Bend National Park. The dark red fruits are globular and less than $1/2$ inch in diameter.

The brown-flowered cactus is common throughout Big Bend National Park except for the highest elevations of the Chisos Mountains.

BROWN-FLOWERED CACTUS

BROWN-FLOWERED CACTUS
CAUGHT BY LATE SNOWFALL

The Genus *Echinocereus*

Claret cup cactus
(Echinocereus coccineus)

The claret cups were previously classified as *E. triglochidiatus*.

Claret cup stems are usually branched from several to many times, sometimes forming dense mounds. The individual branches may reach 10 inches in length and 4 inches in diameter. The spines are tan or gray or pinkish and are sparse, revealing the shiny green surface of the stem.

Claret cup flowers are brilliant orange-red, almost fluorescent, and up to about 3 inches in diameter. They bloom in April and May. The cylindrical red fruits are about an inch long.

Claret cups are cactuses of uplands and woodlands and are common in Big Bend National Park above 4,000 feet. They favor, but are not restricted to, soils of volcanic origins. They occur on rocky or grassy hillsides and are common in juniper-pinyon and oak woodlands.

This species has been variously subdivided into varieties. The taxonomy of *E. coccineus* continues to be studied and refined.

CLARET CUP CACTUS

The Genus *Echinocereus*

Texas rainbow cactus
(Echinocereus dasyacanthus)

The stems of the Texas rainbow (also called Texas pitaya) are usually solitary, although they may occasionally branch once or twice. These spiny cylinders may reach as much as 12 inches in height and up to 4 inches in diameter. The dense spines obscure the stems; they vary in color from white to gray to pink or brown. On some individuals, each year's new spines make a distinct band around the plant. The result is a stem with alternating bands of color, vaguely suggesting a rainbow.

The showy flowers of the rainbow cactus vary from about $2^1/2$ to 4 inches in diameter and are usually bright lemon yellow, but some may be orange to pinkish. They bloom in April and May. The fruits are green, sometimes with a purple tinge, and up to $2^1/2$ inches long.

The Texas rainbow is locally abundant on limestone hills up to about 5,000 feet in elevation.

TEXAS RAINBOW CACTUS

The Genus *Echinocereus*

Strawberry hedgehog
(Echinocereus enneacanthus)

The stems of the strawberry hedgehog branch profusely with up to 100 or more stems in great loose clumps. The individual stems are up to 12 inches long and 4 inches in diameter. The straw to gray spines are quite variable in density, ranging from thick to sparse.

The flowers are magenta and up to 4 inches across, and usually bloom from March through May. The ripe fruits are purplish red and about 2 inches long. The spines on the fruits are loosely attached and easily removed. These fruits are often referred to by their Mexican name, pitaya.

Two varieties of strawberry hedgehog are described for Big Bend National Park. We may distinguish them primarily on the basis of the density of the clusters and the elevation where they grow. *E. e.* var. *enneacanthus* occurs at low elevations on open clay flats in the vicinity of the Rio Grande and forms very loose open clusters. *E. e.* var. *dubius* occurs up to the intermediate elevations such as those of Tornillo Flats, has sparse spines that do not obscure the stems, and forms clumps somewhat more compact than those of var. *enneacanthus*.

STRAWBERRY HEDGEHOG

The Genus *Echinocereus*

Strawberry cactus
(Echinocereus stramineus)

« 32 » The strawberry cactus has also been classified as a variety of
E. enneacanthus, but now is usually ranked as a distinct
species. It forms large, dense, domelike mounds up to 3 feet
in diameter and nearly 3 feet high. The straw-colored spines
obscure the stems.

The flowers are brilliant magenta and up to 4 inches across.
A large plant may bear over 100 flowers. The mature fruits are
purplish red and about 2 inches long. These fleshy fruits are
edible and delicious, tasting similar to fresh strawberries.

Strawberry cactus is common in Big Bend on open slopes
up to about 5,300 feet elevation.

STRAWBERRY CACTUS

The Genus *Echinocereus*

The Genus *Echinomastus*
PINEAPPLE CACTUSES

Botanists differ in their classification of the pineapple cactuses. You will find them variously placed in the genera *Echinocactus*, *Sclerocactus*, and *Neolloydia*.

The egg-shaped stems of this genus remind some observers of miniature pineapples, hence the common name. The stems are under 6 inches in length. The spines are very dense, virtually concealing the surfaces of the stems. The flowers and fruits are produced on recent growth near the tips of the stems. Three species of *Echinomastus* occur in Big Bend National Park.

Chihuahua pineapple cactus
(Echinomastus intertextus)

Some of the egg-shaped stems are elevated above the ground level on a pedestallike tap root. Stems are about 3 to 6 inches long. The spines are pinkish to grayish and dense, obscuring the surface of the stems.

The flowers are white to pale pink. The prominent stigmas are conspicuously red. The flowers are about $1^{1}/_{4}$ inches in diameter. The pineapple cactus is among the very early bloomers; flowers appear in February and March. The mature fruits are dry and tan or brown and about $^{1}/_{2}$ inch long.

The pineapple cactus occurs in grassland habitats, in gravel soils, usually around 3,000 to 4,000 feet in elevation.

CHIHUAHUA PINEAPPLE CACTUS

The Genus *Echinomastus*

Mariposa cactus
(Echinomastus mariposensis)

The egg-shaped stems of the Mariposa cactus are commonly about the size of a golf ball, but may grow to about $3\frac{1}{2}$ inches tall and up to 2 inches in diameter. The whitish radial spines are so dense that they completely obscure the surface of the stems. A prominent bluish gray or brownish central spine stands outright from the stem.

The flowers are about an inch in diameter and bloom in February and March. The petals are pink to white with distinct greenish to reddish purple midribs. The stigmas are green. The yellowish globose fruits are about $\frac{1}{2}$ inch in diameter.

The Mariposa cactus occurs on limestone hills below 3,500 feet elevation, primarily in the eastern sections of Big Bend National Park. It was named for the Mariposa Mine at Terlingua, west of the park.

MARIPOSA
CACTUS

The Genus *Echinomastus*

Warnock cactus
(Echinomastus warnockii)

The solitary bluish green stems of the Warnock cactus are commonly about 4 inches tall, but occasionally may reach nearly 6 inches. The spines are quite dense, nearly obscuring the stems. The prominent central spines are tan with purplish to brown tips.

Warnock cactus flowers are white, sometimes with a pinkish blush. They are about 1 inch in diameter and begin to bloom in February. The round green fruits, less than $^1/_2$ inch in diameter, become brownish at maturity.

The Warnock cactus is locally common throughout much of Big Bend National Park below 4,000 feet in elevation. It was named for Dr. Barton H. Warnock, a longtime professor of biology at Sul Ross State University in Alpine, Texas, and the very popular and respected dean of Big Bend botanists.

WARNOCK CACTUS

The Genus *Echinomastus*

The Genus *Epithelantha*
BUTTON CACTUSES

The button cactuses are aptly named; the tiny globose stems, with their dense coats of minute spines, are truly buttonlike. The stems are usually solitary, but occasionally branch and may even form clumps. They rarely exceed 2 inches in height and commonly have a flattened top. The spines are so tiny and lie so flat that they can be touched without discomfort. The flowers and fruits occur on new growth of the current season, at the very tips of the stems. The flowers are white to pink and up to almost $1/2$ inch in diameter. They bloom from May through August, depending on rainfall. The club-shaped fruits are less than an inch long and are bright red. The button cactuses occur mostly on limestone and at the lower elevations of Big Bend National Park. Some cactologists question whether the button cactuses of Big Bend National Park are but two varieties of the same species or are actually two distinct species.

Boke button cactus
(Epithelantha bokei)

« 38 »   The Boke button cactus is very similar to the common button
cactus but has a smoother, tidier overall image. The tiny flatly
appressed spines present a satiny appearance. The pinkish
flowers barely exceed $^1/_4$ inch in diameter. This button cactus
was named for Dr. Norman H. Boke, University of Oklahoma,
who collected it first in 1955.

BOKE BUTTON CACTUS

The Genus *Epithelantha*

BOKE BUTTON CACTUS IN FRUIT

The Genus *Epithelantha*

Common button cactus
(Epithelantha micromeris)

The common button cactus may be distinguished by a tuft of longer spines on the younger growth at the apex of the stem. This spine tuft may even obscure the tiny flowers. The bright red fruits, however, are conspicuous. The common button cactus is usually found on low limestone ridges, but it has been recorded in the Chisos Mountains. (Not illustrated)

The Genus *Epithelantha*

The Genus *Ferocactus*
BARREL CACTUSES

Most barrel cactuses are large columnar plants, such as the familiar barrels of the Sonoran Desert in Arizona. Some, however, are much smaller, such as our one example in Big Bend National Park. The stems are prominently ribbed and bear conspicuous tubercles. The genus name, *Ferocactus*, means "fierce" or "ferocious cactus," an apt reference to the heavy, sharp, and sometimes hooked spines. The flowers and fruits occur on the new growth of the current season, near the tip of the stem. The fruits of barrel cactuses are fleshy at maturity.

Texas barrel cactus
(Ferocactus hamatacanthus)

The Texas barrel is one of the smaller members of the barrel cactuses. The stems rarely exceed 12 inches in length and 6 inches in diameter. They are usually solitary but may occur in large many-stemmed clumps. Because of its conspicuous, giant, hooked central spines, this cactus is sometimes called giant fishhook cactus. These straw-colored spines can get to be 4 inches long.

The flowers are yellow with reddish centers and are up to 3 inches in diameter. They form a cluster around the apex of the stem. The fleshy green fruits ripen to brownish red and are a little more than an inch long.

The Texas barrel cactus is locally abundant in cliffs and rocky hillsides from the Rio Grande up to about 5,000 feet elevation.

TEXAS BARREL CACTUS

The Genus *Ferocactus*

The Genus *Glandulicactus*
FISHHOOK CACTUSES

These small barrellike cactuses are solitary, nearly globose to egg-shaped, and up to about 6 inches in height. The lowest central spine is long and hooked. The flowers and fruits occur on the new growth of the current season, near the tips of the stems.

Wright fishhook cactus
(Glandulicactus uncinatus var. wrightii)

This cactus has also been classified in the genus *Ancistrocactus* by some botanists.

The solitary stems of the Wright fishhook cactus rarely exceed 6 inches in height. The abundant yellowish to reddish spines do not obscure the dark green stems. The principal central spine, up to 4 inches long, is strongly hooked and usually turned upward. When viewed from a distance, these spines give Wright fishhook cactus the appearance of a clump of grass.

The orange-brown flowers are about 1 to $1^{1}/4$ inches in diameter and grow in a tight circle around the apex of the stem. They usually bloom from March through June. The egg-shaped reddish fruits are about an inch long.

The Wright fishhook cactus is widespread, but not common, throughout Big Bend National Park below 4,000 feet elevation.

WRIGHT FISHHOOK CACTUS

The Genus *Glandulicactus*

The Genus *Mammillaria*
NIPPLE CACTUSES

The generic name *Mammillaria* is derived from the Latin *mamma*, which means "breast" or "nipple." It refers to the nipplelike tubercles on the stems. The flowers and fruits occur on old growth of the preceding season, and thus grow in a ring around the tip of the stem. This is a very large genus, but only three species are known to occur in Big Bend National Park.

Heyder pincushion cactus
(Mammillaria heyderi)

The dark green stem of the pincushion cactus is a low hemisphere with a flattened or depressed top. It commonly attains a diameter of 6 inches. The spines, growing at the tips of the prominent tubercles, are not dense and do not obscure the surfaces of the stems.

The flowers grow in a neat circle around the apex of the stem. They are cream to pinkish and about an inch in diameter. They bloom from March through June. The fruits are about $1/2$ to $1\,1/4$ inches long.

The Heyder pincushion cactus occurs commonly throughout much of Big Bend National Park below 5,300 feet elevation. Two virtually indistinguishable varieties occur in the park: *M. h.* var. *heyderi* has a more flattened stem tip, reddish fruits, and may be found more commonly below 4,500 feet elevation; *M. h.* var. *meiacantha* has a more rounded stem form, rosy purplish fruits, and usually occurs from 4,000 to 5,300 feet elevation. This cactus was named for the German cactologist Heyder (1804–1884).

HEYDER PINCUSHION CACTUS

Lacespine cactus
(Mammillaria lasiacantha)

« 48 » The tiny globular stems of the lacespine cactus are usually less than 1 1/2 inches in diameter. They resemble golf balls, so this cactus is sometimes referred to as the golf ball cactus. The fine white spines are very dense, completely obscuring the stems. The lacespine cactus can easily be confused with the button cactuses, *Epithelantha micromeris*. They can be found growing together.

The flower petals are whitish with reddish brown midstripes. The flowers are about 1/2 inch across and bloom from March through May. The bright scarlet fruits are about 1/2 inch long.

The lacespine cactus is very inconspicuous in its matching limestone habitat. It is fairly common at the lower elevations of Big Bend National Park.

LACESPINE CACTUS

The Genus *Mammillaria*

Potts mammillaria
(Mammillaria pottsii)

The stems of the Potts mammillaria may be solitary, but are commonly branched into clusters of several to many. They are long and thin, 8 by $1^{1}/_{4}$ inches, and so this beautiful plant has been ignominiously called rattail and foxtail cactus. The radial spines are white and very dense, obscuring the stems. The centrals are dark purplish or brownish, with one prominently curved upward.

The reddish maroon bell-shaped flowers open to only about $^{1}/_{2}$ inch in diameter. They grow in a ring below the stem apex, on old plant growth, and bloom from March through May. The fruits are red and fleshy and about $^{1}/_{2}$ inch long.

The Potts mammillaria occurs in limestone soils at the lower elevations of Big Bend National Park and is widespread in Mexico, but occurs nowhere else in the United States.

POTTS MAMMILLARIA

The Genus *Mammillaria*

The Genus *Neolloydia*

LLOYD STOUT-SPINED CACTUSES

This genus was named to honor botanist Francis E. Lloyd (1868–1947). Some cactologists do not recognize the genus *Neolloydia*, preferring to classify these plants in the stout-spined cactus genus, *Echinocactus*, or in *Echinomastus*, the pineapple cactuses.

The stems of *Neolloydia* are either ovoid or cylindrical, usually no more than about 5 inches long, and may be either solitary or branched into clumps. The magenta flowers and fruits occur on new growth of the current season, so they are located at the tips of the stems. The fruits are dry at maturity.

Texas cone cactus
(Neolloydia conoidea)

The stems of the Texas cone cactus are sometimes solitary, but commonly branch into clumps up to 12 inches across. They seldom exceed 4 to 5 inches in height. The spines are fairly dense but do not obscure the stems. The central spines are blackish when young but turn gray with age. The radial spines are white.

The flowers are magenta to purple and up to 2 inches in diameter, usually blooming in May and June. The small round fruits are yellowish at first but mature to dry and brown.

The Texas cone cactus occurs on limestone slopes, below 4,000 feet elevation, in the eastern portions of Big Bend National Park.

TEXAS CONE CACTUS

The Genus *Opuntia*
CHOLLAS AND PRICKLYPEARS

The genus *Opuntia* (oh-PUNCH-ya) is a very large and distinctive group of cactuses. The branched stems are composed of chains of connected joints, and the areoles bear numerous minute, sharp, barbed bristles called glochids. Always be careful when touching the stems or fruits of chollas or pricklypears as these glochids can be extremely irritating and difficult to remove from the skin. The young growing pads bear small, fleshy, cylindrical leaves, but these fall by the end of the first growth season.

The stem joints of chollas (CHOY-ahs) are cylindrical, round in cross section. Pricklypear joints are flattened and are commonly referred to as pads.

It is particularly difficult to identify chollas and pricklypears due to the great variation within a species and the strong tendencies for species to hybridize. Distinct characters are often difficult to associate with a species. Specialists in the genus *Opuntia* are continually describing new species and revising earlier classifications.

The pricklypears are an economically important group. Sometimes the spines are burned off so cattle can eat the pads. And the young tender pads, called nopalitos, are commonly boiled or breaded with cornmeal and fried for human consumption. Look for canned nopalitos in West Texas grocery stores. The fruits—the pears—of many species are juicy, sweet, and edible. In Mexico they are called tunas.

The genus name, *Opuntia*, was first used by the ancient Greek botanist Theophrastus (371–287 B.C.) for a completely different plant and refers to the old Greek town of Opus. The name was given to this group of cactuses by the French botanist Joseph Pitton de Tournefort (1656–1708) for reasons not clearly understood.

The Genus *Opuntia*

Golden-spined pricklypear
(Opuntia aureispina)

« 54 » The golden-spined pricklypear is an upright shrub, with a distinct trunk, up to about 5 feet high. The trunk is densely covered with spines. The pads are bluish to yellowish green and are about 3 to 4 3/4 inches broad and long. The areoles bear 4 to 12 spines, which are often twisted and up to about 2 1/2 inches long.

   The golden-spined pricklypear blooms in March and April. The flowers are yellow with bright orange or red centers and are about 2 1/2 inches in diameter. The mature fruits are dry and spiny.

   This pricklypear grows in rocky limestone soils below 2,000 feet elevation. It is very rare in Big Bend National Park. It may also occur southward in Mexico.

GOLDEN-SPINED PRICKLYPEAR

The Genus *Opuntia*

Texas pricklypear
(Opuntia chisosensis)

The Texas pricklypear may be either a sprawling or an upright shrub up to 5 feet high or, rarely, more. The plants may be solitary or may grow in large thickets. The pads are green and up to nearly 1 inch thick, 8 inches broad, and 10 inches long. The areoles bear 1 to 6 yellow spines and yellow glochids that turn brown with age.

Texas pricklypear blooms in May and June. Its flowers are usually waxy yellow but occasionally red. The purple fruit, up to about 2 1/2 inches long, is fleshy at maturity and falls from the plant when it ripens.

This pricklypear occurs in sandy-gravelly soils on plains and hillsides up to about 5,500 feet elevation.

The Texas pricklypear is very similar to Engelmann pricklypear (*O. engelmannii*). Some cactologists believe they should be classified as varieties of the same species.

TEXAS PRICKLYPEAR

The Genus *Opuntia*

Engelmann pricklypear
(Opuntia engelmannii)

For a long time Engelmann pricklypear was known to many botanists as *O. phaeacantha* var. *discata*. There is a trend now to revert to *O. engelmannii*. You will find both names in publications.

Engelmann pricklypear forms a large shrub of creeping, prostrate stems that spread widely at ground level, often with numerous rooted stems forming a colony without definite trunk or basal stem. The plants are usually about 4 to 6 feet

ENGELMANN PRICKLYPEAR

COW'S TONGUE PRICKLYPEAR

tall and the colonies up to about 30 feet in diameter. The blue-green pads are oblong to circular, 7 to 10 inches across, and up to 12 inches long. The widely spaced areoles each hold 1 to 5 white to grayish spines, which are up to about $2^{1}/_{2}$ inches long and pointed downward.

The flowers are yellow with bright green stigmas and are about $2^{1}/_{2}$ to 4 inches in diameter. The juicy fruits, called tunas, are rich burgundy in color and are edible. They are commonly harvested for making syrups and jellies and are an important food item in Mexico.

Not only is Engelmann one of the largest pricklypears, it is widespread and common throughout most of the desert Southwest and is abundant in Big Bend National Park.

An odd variety of this species, cow's tongue pricklypear (*O. e.* var. *linguiformis*), was introduced into the Big Bend country by pioneer families for landscaping around their homes. A few persist around some of these old homestead sites to this day. They are distinguished by their elongate, lance-shaped (cow's tongue) pads, which may reach 3 feet in length.

The Genus *Opuntia*

Graham club cholla
(Opuntia grahamii)

The Graham club cholla is one of the club chollas, discussed below under Schott club cholla (*O. schottii*). These two small chollas are very similar and can be difficult for park visitors to distinguish in the field.

The stem joints of *O. grahamii* are $1^{1}/4$ to $1^{3}/4$ inches long. There may be 7 to 14 spines per areole, and they are 1 to $1^{1}/2$ inches long, round in cross section. There is no distinct central spine.

The flowers, about $1^{1}/2$ inches across, are yellow. The outer petals have a central pink tinge. The stamen filaments are yellow-green. The Graham club cholla blooms in May and June.

GRAHAM CLUB CHOLLA

The Genus *Opuntia*

Cane cholla
(Opuntia imbricata)

This large shrublike cholla, sometimes called tree cactus, may reach heights of 6 feet with a distinct basal trunk to 4 inches in diameter. The stem joints are about 6 to 8 inches long and 1 to 1 1/2 inches in diameter and covered with prominent elongated tubercles. The oval areoles bear 10 to 30 whitish to brown spines that are about 1 1/4 inches long.

CANE CHOLLA

The purplish lavender flowers, up to 3 inches in diameter, bloom from April through June. The knobby yellow fruits may exceed 1 1/2 inches in length and usually remain on the plants throughout the winter.

Cane cholla grows commonly in gravelly or sandy soils throughout much of Big Bend National Park, especially between 4,000 to 6,000 feet. Doves, cactus wrens, and other birds build their nests in the sturdy spiny branches of cane cholla.

A unique Big Bend variety of cane cholla is silverspine cane cholla (*O. i.* var. *argentea*). Shorter than cane cholla, this cholla rarely reaches 4 feet in height. Its dense silvery spines give this plant a distinct appearance. The range of this cholla is very limited, growing only on the dry slopes of Mariscal Mountain and other nearby limestone hills and probably in adjacent Mexico. It is also called Mariscal cholla and Big Bend cane cholla.

SILVERSPINE CHOLLA

The Genus *Opuntia*

Klein cholla
(Opuntia kleiniae)

The Klein cholla, also called candle cholla, is a many-branched shrub that grows to about 6 feet in height. The very slender joints are 4 to 12 inches in length and about $^1/_2$ inch in diameter; some may have a purplish red tinge. The widely spaced areoles each bear 1 to 4 spines, each covered with a loose light tan sheath.

The flowers are pale greenish purple with a distinct bronze tone. They are about 1 to $1^1/_4$ inches in diameter and usually bloom in May and June. The orange-red fruits, about 1 to $1^1/_4$ inches long, persist on the plant through the winter.

In Big Bend National Park the Klein cholla grows only at low elevations along the Rio Grande in sandy-gravelly soils.

KLEIN CHOLLA

The Genus *Opuntia*

Desert Christmas cholla
(Opuntia leptocaulis)

In Mexico and West Texas this plant is called tasajillo (tah-sah-HEE-yo). It is a very slender sprawling to upright bush that seldom exceeds 3 feet in height. The thin joints are $^1/_4$ to $^1/_2$ inch in diameter and up to a foot long. Most areoles bear a single spine that may reach 2 inches in length and is covered with a loose-fitting, papery white-tan sheath.

The greenish white flowers are about 1 inch in diameter and bloom from April to July. The bright orange-red pear-shaped fruits are up to 1 inch in length and decorate the plant through most of the winter, hence the name desert Christmas cholla.

Tasajillo is found throughout Big Bend National Park below 5,000 feet elevation. It is common in washes and open flats and often grows in the protection of larger plants such as creosotebush and mesquite.

DESERT CHRISTMAS CHOLLA

The Genus *Opuntia*

DESERT CHRISTMAS CHOLLA IN FRUIT

The Genus *Opuntia*

PAD OF PURPLE PRICKLYPEAR

The Genus *Opuntia*

Purple pricklypear
(Opuntia macrocentra)

This sprawling shrub is less than 3 feet high. The stems are conspicuously purplish, especially in winter and after prolonged periods of drought. The pads are nearly round and up to 7 inches in diameter. The spines occur only in those areoles along the upper margin of the pad, 1 to 2 per areole, up to about 6 inches in length and black, but sometimes turning whitish with age.

The gorgeous flowers are yellow with conspicuous bright red centers and get to be 3 $1/2$ inches in diameter. They bloom in April and May. The fruits are reddish purple, fleshy at maturity, and persist on the stems until November.

The purple pricklypear is common in Big Bend National Park in sandy soils and gravelly slopes below 4,000 feet elevation.

PURPLE PRICKLYPEAR

The Genus *Opuntia*

Plains pricklypear
(*Opuntia macrorhiza*)

This grasslands pricklypear is a low spreading shrub commonly growing in clumps and often obscured by grasses. The bluish pads are about $2^{1}/_{2}$ inches wide and 4 inches long. There are 1 to 6 whitish spines per areole, occurring mostly in the uppermost areoles of the pads. Glochids are yellow or brown.

The flowers are yellow with reddish centers and up to $2^{1}/_{4}$ inches wide. The reddish purple fruits may persist on the plants for several months.

Plains pricklypear occurs in gravelly-rocky soils and in grasslands and woodlands up to 7,000 feet elevation.

PLAINS PRICKLYPEAR IN GRASSLAND HABITAT. *Photo by Ro Wauer.*

Purplefruit pricklypear
(Opuntia phaeacantha)

The purplefruit pricklypears are large, prostrate, sprawling shrubs that often form clumps over 10 feet in diameter. The stem pads may reach 8 inches in width and 12 inches in length. Spines may occur in all areoles or only in those on the upper portions of the pads. Glochids vary in color from yellowish tan to brown.

The flowers vary from yellow to orange to red and are about 3 inches in diameter. The fruits are purple, fleshy when mature, and edible; they may reach almost 3 inches in length. They remain on the plants until winter. These fruits are relished by many birds and mammals as well as by people.

Cactus specialists disagree over just which pricklypears should be included in this species (note earlier comments on *O. engelmannii*). Some have split the species into several varieties based on pad size, distribution of spines on the pads, spine color and length, and so forth. Others feel these deserve to be ranked as distinct species. Furthermore, the varieties tend to hybridize and intergrade with each other, thus adding to our confusion when we try to identify them in the field. As stated earlier, the Engelmann pricklypear has been, and still is, classified by some taxonomists as *O. p.* var. *discata*. (Not illustrated)

Blind pricklypear
(Opuntia rufida)

This erect pricklypear may reach a height of 5 feet. Its oval to round grayish green pads are up to 6 inches in diameter. It has no spines. The areoles are filled with conspicuous, loosely attached, reddish brown glochids that fly when the plants are jarred or blown by strong winds. According to southwestern folklore, these glochids are capable of blinding cattle, hence its common name.

The flowers of blind pricklypear are about 3 inches in diameter and are yellow, then turn orange with age. They bloom in April and May. The fruits are red, about an inch long, are fleshy at maturity, and do not remain on the plant for very long.

The blind pricklypear occurs in sandy to gravelly soils and hillsides throughout Big Bend National Park, mostly below 4,000 feet elevation.

BLIND PRICKLYPEAR

The Genus *Opuntia*

Schott club cholla
(Opuntia schottii)

Plant taxonomists continue to study, debate, and reclassify the low, mat-forming cactuses, known as the club chollas or dog chollas. The original common name was dog turd cholla, a reference to its supposed appearance, as well as its tendency to cling to shoes. The name has been properly shortened to suit modern sensibilities. For many years, some classified them all as a single species, *O. schottii*. Some others distinguished a variety: *O. schottii* var. *grahamii*. Still others argue that these are two distinct species: *O. schottii* and *O. grahamii*, and they are so treated here.

The club chollas form low, ground-hugging mats up to 10 feet in diameter but are seldom more than about 4 inches high. The stem joints are prostrate and usually club-shaped, thickening near the tips to nearly 1 inch in diameter. The long sharp spines easily penetrate hikers' boots, causing the joints to break off. When left on the ground, these joints readily take root to form new plants.

O. schottii has joints that are $1^3/4$ to $2^1/2$ inches long. There are 8 to 14 spines per areole, which are $1^1/2$ to $2^1/2$ inches long, flattened in cross section, and reddish brown, with a distinct central spine.

The flowers, which bloom in June and July, are bright lemon yellow and up to about $1^1/2$ inches across. The outer petals have a central pink tinge; stamen filaments are yellow. The fleshy yellow fruits often persist on plants until the following year.

The club chollas occur commonly in loosely consolidated soils on gentle gravelly slopes and sandy flats throughout Big Bend National Park below 5,000 feet elevation.

CLUB OR DOG CHOLLA

The Genus *Opuntia*

Spinyfruit pricklypear
(Opuntia spinosibacca)

The erect stems of this pricklypear may reach 4 feet in height. The pear-shaped pads are about 4 to 6 inches wide and 4 to 7 inches long. The areoles occur on unusual small elevations on the surfaces of the pads. There are usually from 1 to 5 dark heavy spines per areole.

The flowers, up to 2 inches in diameter, are yellow to orange with red centers. The spiny fruits are greenish yellow when mature.

The spinyfruit pricklypear is locally common in gravelly soils and desert flats below 3,000 feet elevation.

Spinyfruit pricklypear is believed to be a hybrid, possibly a cross between golden-spined pricklypear (*O. aureispina*) and purplefruit pricklypear (*O. phaeacantha*).

SPINYFRUIT PRICKLYPEAR

The Genus *Opuntia*

The Genus *Thelocactus*
TEXAS NIPPLE CACTUSES

Thelo is derived from the Greek word for
"breast" and refers to the nipplelike tubercles
on the plant stems The tubercles merge
tightly together, separated by only slitlike
lines. The flowers and fruits occur at the
apex of the stems on the new growth of the
current season. The genus *Thelocactus*
occurs only in Mexico and Texas. One
species grows in Big Bend National Park.

Glory of Texas
(Thelocactus bicolor)

The stems of glory of Texas are solitary, grayish blue-green, and usually egg-shaped. They may reach 8 inches in height and 4 or 5 inches in diameter. The long central spines are flattened and flexible, white and pink-red in color, and get up to 3 inches or more in length.

The spectacular flowers are a brilliant satiny fuschia with deep scarlet throats, often growing to 4 inches in diameter. They bloom from April through June. The fruits are about $^{1}/_{2}$ inch long and are green and dry at maturity.

The variety of this species that occurs in Big Bend National Park is *T. b.* var. *schottii*, named for Arthur Schott, a geologist who also collected plants for the Emory Survey of the U.S.-Mexico Boundary from 1851 to 1853. The glory of Texas is primarily a Mexican species and is not common in Big Bend National Park. It occurs at a few isolated locations in gravelly and clay soils at lower elevations.

GLORY OF TEXAS

The Genus *Thelocactus*

Other Possibilities

The following are cactus species that have been reported in Big Bend National Park in the past but have not been confirmed in recent years.

Barrel cactus
(Ferocactus wislizenii)

This massive columnar cactus is the common barrel cactus of the Sonoran Desert in Arizona. The yellow to orange flowers bloom from June through September. This barrel cactus was introduced into the Big Bend country by early residents for ornamentals around their homes. A few may still survive, but it has not been reported in the park recently.

BARREL CACTUS

Peyote
(Lophophora williamsii)

« 78 » The dull bluish green stems of peyote may be solitary or clustered. The low hemispheres may reach about 4 inches in diameter. They are spineless. The pink flowers, up to an inch across, bloom in May and June. Peyote has not been confirmed in Big Bend National Park in recent years. The early reports were usually near the sites of prehistoric campsites. It is possible that these were introduced by Indians who used it in religious ceremonies for its hallucinatory effects.

PEYOTE

Other Possibilities

Dark-spined pricklypear
(Opuntia atrispina)

This relatively small sprawling pricklypear has black spines with yellow tips. The yellow flowers, to $2^{1}/_{2}$ inches across, bloom in April and May. It is uncommon, and its occurrence within Big Bend National Park is uncertain. (Not illustrated)

Other Possibilities

Night-blooming cereus
(Peniocereus greggii)

The long, slender, inconspicuous stems of the night-blooming cereus grow among protective shrubs, such as creosotebush. The spectacular white flowers bloom at night during June. It is known to have occurred in Big Bend National Park years ago, but there are no confirmed reports from recent years.

NIGHT-BLOOMING CEREUS

Index